YOU ARE ALTOGETHER

beautiful,

MY LOVE; THERE IS
NO FLAW IN YOU.

-Jesus

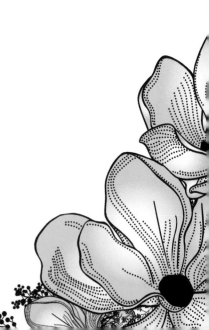

I Am A Woman
Copyright © 2020 by Anu Kasturi
All rights reserved

First Edition
Printed in the United States

Hardcover (Dust): 978-1-64990-186-6
Paperback: 978-1-64990-032-6
eBook: 978-1-64990-031-9

CONTENTS

Introduction 3
Chapter 1: You're Worth It! 8
Chapter 2: You Belong 26
Chapter 3: A-Game Not Needed 50
Chapter 4: Re-start 68
Chapter 5: She Believed! 88
Conclusion 109

INTRODUCTION

This book is dedicated to all women whose circumstances seem to tell them, "You're just a woman." God wants you to strike the word *"just"* from that line because that's not who you are. Although you may have gone through diverse challenges growing up and currently live in a world of indifference, condemnation, and judgment, God wants you to know that no matter the conjectures, stereotypes, or opinions the world has imposed, you're still His beloved daughter; you were fearfully and wonderfully created in His very own image. He sees *"U"* in the *beaUtiful* so don't let the world tell you otherwise.

If people have hurt you and have left you with scars, Jesus wants you to look at His nail-scarred hands and be reminded, as you behold Him, that He took all your scars, nailed them to the cross, and through His precious blood made you forever *flawless*. Let not that hurt break you down and stop you from walking into the blessing that God has already promised. Be confident of this one thing that He who began the good work in you is faithful enough to bring it to fruition.

The blessing the Lord has kept aside for you *will be yours* in His time, and nothing or no one can ever stop you from receiving it. But until that promise comes to pass, don't let those lies trick you into sorrow. Allow Jesus to mend your heart, wipe your tears, embrace you with His loving arms, and heal your brokenness. It's time to shake off the dust, leave the world behind, put Jesus in front of you, and *rise up*! Don't dwell in the haze of the past and fail to enter into the bright beginning that Jesus prepared for you. Know that today is not the end, as there is always a tomorrow. Let not the world steal the real you by imposing its judgment on you. You are *important* to God and He values you for who you are. It doesn't matter where the world leaves you; all that should matter is where *Jesus takes you*, so don't let your past determine the outcome of your future.

You might be operating in different roles every day, and sometimes you might feel that your service is invaluable yet not treasured enough or that your life is not progressing as you wanted it to progress. But isn't it true that being a mother to a child, a wife to a husband, a sister to a sibling, a daughter to a family, and serving at different capacities in different roles has allowed God to demonstrate to you that you are valuable and chosen for a reason beyond your service and practical roles?

The many hats that women wear might not always seem rewarding, but without those roles, life itself might not seem to emerge as God intended it to be. So no matter who you are, where you're from, or what you do, always know that you are the "child of the Most High God." Let not the devil steal your thunder because your smile can bring joy, your eyes can spark life, your aura can brighten your surroundings, and your presence can make a difference. You're not just a woman. You are a woman, and you matter to God.

...I'VE CALLED YOUR NAME. YOU'RE MINE. WHEN YOU'RE IN OVER YOUR HEAD, I'LL BE THERE WITH YOU. WHEN YOU'RE IN ROUGH WATERS, YOU WILL NOT GO DOWN. WHEN YOU'RE BETWEEN A ROCK AND A HARD PLACE, IT WON'T BE A DEAD END - BECAUSE I AM GOD, YOUR PERSONAL GOD, THE HOLY OF ISRAEL, YOUR SAVIOR. I PAID A HUGE PRICE FOR YOU...

THAT'S HOW MUCH YOU MEAN TO ME!
THAT'S HOW MUCH I LOVE YOU! I'D SELL
OFF THE WHOLE WORLD TO GET YOU BACK,
TRADE THE CREATION JUST FOR YOU.

ISAIAH 43:1-4, MSG

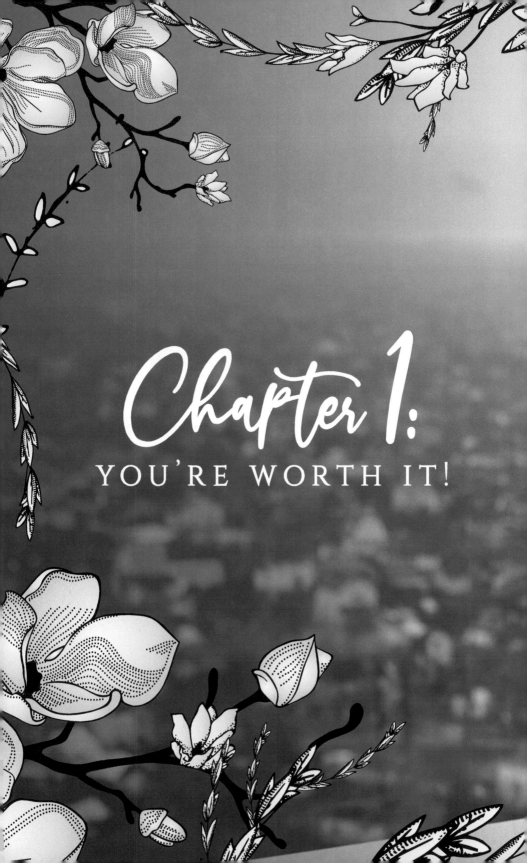

Chapter 1:
YOU'RE WORTH IT!

You're worth it! I love this line so very much. Sometimes I secretly go into my bedroom, stand in front of the mirror, and say this line. It has definitely brought a smile and some measure of confidence whenever I've said it. This line truly represents the value of every single woman created by God. We're all created beautifully, artistically, and wonderfully by the Most High God. Just knowing that *I'm worth every single second* of God's time and *every single thought* behind His handiwork gives me so much more confidence than I would otherwise have to face the world every single day.

OH YES, YOU SHAPED ME FIRST
INSIDE, THEN OUT; YOU FORMED
ME IN MY MOTHER'S WOMB.
I THANK YOU, HIGH GOD—
YOU'RE BREATHTAKING! BODY
AND SOUL, I AM MARVELOUSLY
MADE! I WORSHIP IN
ADORATION—WHAT A CREATION!

PSALM 139:13–14, MSG

God took the time to uniquely create each one of us. He definitely put so much thought into the process of creation, whether to intricately design each cell, each nerve, every part of our bodies or to embed those characteristics that are different yet fully realized in each of us. Unless we believe in the fact that we're *"marvelously made"* in *"body and soul,"* we cannot truly reflect the beauty of the inner being that God put in us. He wants us to know that although each one of us is unique all of our hearts are knit together by His spirit, and it is *heart* that matters to Him more than appearance.

Sometimes it's easier to say, "Oh, yes! Jesus made me beautiful in every which way." But it's harder to believe it because we step into a world of condemnation and judgment every single day, whether we want it or not; that's the reality of life. In those moments when insecurity rises to the level of dissatisfaction, our whole world starts to crumble. We then start comparing ourselves with others and start feeling bad about how we look, how we talk, how we behave, and in fact start disliking everything about ourselves. We'll then measure our worth by the worldly scale, feel insecure, and start saying things like "I don't think I'll look good in this dress" or "I wish I was slim, fair, and tall like her" or "I don't think I'm made for this." The list goes on and on and on.

We categorize our identities based on some kind of varying, absurd checklist and try to fit into the options on that list. We need to understand that our value lies beyond those irrelevant stereotypes. The God of the universe calls us sanctified, purified, holy, set apart, worthy, flawless, glorious, beautiful, and marvelous. This is who we are; *what He calls us is who we are!* Our stories are not written by the world but by God.

When we become vulnerable to the lies, the enemy builds a wall around us, and sometimes it's not even the enemy we fight but the walls around us. We keep building the walls by believing in the lies, and unless we start letting God overtake our thoughts, we can never get beyond the walls. The enemy only knows how to start a thought but has no control over how we process it. If we foster the lies, we will slowly slip into disappointment and doubt God's purpose, and that's exactly what the enemy wants. The only way those walls can break is by believing in God's truth.

Mary, the mother of Jesus, had to deal with so many walls while living out her purpose. When the world made her feel lowly and unknown, God exalted her by choosing her among all women to give birth to the savior of the world. Even in her wildest imagination she must never have thought that she would be holding the one who would save the world, but God *chose* her anyway. A woman who was solely confined to household chores growing up was chosen by God for the most important, glorious, and extravagant miracle ever known to mankind.

> ## AND HAVING COME IN, THE ANGEL SAID TO HER, "REJOICE, HIGHLY FAVORED ONE, THE LORD IS WITH YOU; BLESSED ARE YOU AMONG WOMEN!"
>
> **LUKE 1:28, NKJV**

The way the Lord addresses Mary is itself so touching. By addressing her as favored and blessed, He honors her. He sees Mary as worthy of all His blessings and reminds her of her worth by calling her *blessed*. The Lord doesn't look at you the way the world looks at you. It's one thing to be blessed and another to be called blessed. It's like your very own name—when someone addresses you as a "blessed woman," that's who you are.

Mary's beauty was never mentioned as a qualification; her heart for God was the only thing that qualified her. What we call beauty is not what He calls it. Beauty is the reflection of the heart that *personifies His nature* in us. When the angel tells Mary that she will conceive by the power of the Holy Spirit and gives assurance that no Word of God will ever fail, Mary, even though she is scared, still chooses to believe in the words spoken by the angel and claim her promise.

"I AM THE LORD'S SERVANT,"
MARY ANSWERED.
"MAY YOUR WORD TO ME BE FULFILLED."
THEN THE ANGEL LEFT HER.

LUKE 1:38, NIV

Mary doesn't try to wrap her mind around the practical implications of the announcement; instead she holds onto her promise with total submission. When we go through circumstances that make absolutely no sense to us, can we trust God and ask, "May your word be fulfilled"?

AND IT HAPPENED, WHEN ELIZABETH
HEARD THE GREETING OF MARY,
THAT THE BABE LEAPED IN HER WOMB;
AND ELIZABETH WAS FILLED WITH
THE HOLY SPIRIT. THEN SHE SPOKE
OUT WITH A LOUD VOICE AND SAID,
"BLESSED ARE YOU AMONG WOMEN,
AND BLESSED IS THE FRUIT
OF YOUR WOMB!"

LUKE 1:41–42, NKJV

Later, when Mary visits the house of her cousin, Elizabeth, the Lord reminds her again that she is blessed and chosen. At that time Mary doesn't have the visible proof of bearing a child yet, but as she enters, she's reminded again that she's blessed. The Lord wants Mary to own her identity through Him and not through the blessing. She needs to believe that she was truly chosen by God and that's why she's considered "blessed". Just like Mary, we're blessed and highly favored in Christ even when the circumstances don't seem appealing to human rationale or when we don't yet see the blessing. It's not our blessings that define our identity, but the one who blesses us. Jesus made us forever blessed and righteous through His precious blood, and when we confess that we are blessed, we are echoing the truth and trusting Him to turn our lives into a blessing!

AND MARY SAID:
"MY SOUL MAGNIFIES THE LORD,
AND MY SPIRIT HAS REJOICED IN
GOD MY SAVIOR. FOR HE HAS
REGARDED THE LOWLY
STATE OF HIS MAIDSERVANT;
FOR BEHOLD, HENCEFORTH
ALL GENERATIONS WILL CALL ME BLESSED.
FOR HE WHO IS MIGHTY HAS
DONE GREAT THINGS FOR ME,
AND HOLY IS HIS NAME."

LUKE 1:46–49, NKJV

Blessed
Are you among women!

Mary starts praising God for the unseen promise and calls herself blessed because she believes in His words. That's why she was able to embrace her identity as God's blessed child.

Furthermore Elizabeth and Mary each have their own testimonies. Mary doesn't compare herself to her cousin and become anxious about her child. She is content hearing what the Lord has spoken to her and waits on Him. Don't compare yourself with another person and feel discouraged. Never do that! Your testimony is glorious and unique in its own way.

Mary's pregnancy could have been the talk of the town, and she must have faced all kinds of accusations from everyone, but nowhere does the Bible mention any idea of Mary giving up on the promised child. She lives out her purpose by delivering the savior of the world, Jesus Christ. *She makes God her strength and focuses on the purpose* despite the rumors and accusations. Mary was truly a brave woman who lived boldly while ignoring unnecessary distractions because she lived with "God-confidence."

If you're in a similar situation of being judged by people based on the patterns of the world, don't be worried and scared. The world even accused Jesus. So if it can accuse the creator, it can definitely accuse

His creation. Don't listen to the lies of this world. God already chose you and regards you as blessed and worthy. Wherever you go, the Lord will make sure that you are called "blessed." Just believe in His words. Even if the enemy aims the gun at you and pulls the trigger, there is nothing left to harm you because Jesus took all the bullets for you on the cross.

We are living in the new covenant of grace, where our battle has already been won. Our victory lies in just believing in Jesus! It's just not worth fighting. Instead we should know that we're worth the sweet victory that Christ won on that cross. Don't always look at your current position and be dismayed. Rather see how Jesus has already positioned you and be strong. The Lord will rescue you today! Just stand still.

> ...DON'T BE AFRAID. JUST STAND
> STILL AND WATCH
> THE LORD RESCUE YOU
> TODAY. THE EGYPTIANS YOU
> SEE TODAY WILL
> NEVER BE SEEN AGAIN.
>
> EXODUS 14:13, NLT

The most important thing is to have a clear consciousness of who our God is and how much He loves us. Only consciousness of Christ can define the worthiness of our lives. Jesus made us worthy of every victory and every promise. Keep declaring who you are in Christ rather than what state you are in this world.

I hail from a country that is conservative, where Christianity is not so prevalent and widely practiced, from a society where the very purpose of a woman is confined to certain clichés of cultural reasoning. Freedom was not a prerogative; it was a constant fight. Growing up in a world of religious and cultural disparity, it was tough sometimes for me to have the same level of faith and belief as one who knows Jesus is expected to have. My family was very loving, spiritually grounded in the truth and raised me up in God's Word, but that didn't stop the world around me from belittling, humiliating, and making demands on me. I remember questioning God often and being frustrated with life.

But now, if I look back, all I can say is that I'm here today safe and sound because of His grace. Had it not been for Jesus, I wouldn't be here today. He has kept me through all these years. He constantly watched over me, didn't let me slip, and held me close to His heart. Even when I was faithless, doubted, and was far away,

He still became the hand that lifted me up when I fell, He still became the peace when I was stressed, He still became the source of reason when nothing made sense, He still became the path when I lost my way, and He still became everything I ever needed every single moment only because He loved me and He wanted me to be right here, right now. My worth was never devalued because of the way I looked, the way I performed, the way I spoke, the way I dressed, or the way I behaved. His love for me always remained the same because it's forever unwavering, unconditional, and unbiased.

The indelible truth in this whole journey of life is that His purpose will prevail, and His grace will sustain us through all the highs and through all the lows, no matter what! All we need to do is trust Him and wait upon Him. We can only see so much with our eyes, but God sees beyond. He knows the end from the beginning, and He knows exactly what to do, when to do it, and how to do it. He breaks every barrier of burden so we can prosper in His purpose and enjoy the fruits of His blessings. Let us value our lives as Christ values them and trust Him a little more, can we?

BUT YOU ARE THE ONES CHOSEN
BY GOD, CHOSEN FOR THE HIGH CALLING
OF PRIESTLY WORK, CHOSEN
TO BE A HOLY PEOPLE, GOD'S
INSTRUMENTS TO DO HIS WORK
AND SPEAK OUT FOR HIM, TO
TELL OTHERS OF THE NIGHT-
AND-DAY DIFFERENCE HE
MADE FOR YOU—FROM NOTHING
TO SOMETHING, FROM REJECTED
TO ACCEPTED.

1 PETER 2:9–10, MSG

You're accepted by God. Let not the enemy lie to you about rejection in life. You're chosen for a higher calling, just like Mary, and you will prevail if you trust God all the way just as she did. You're His precious daugther and you fully deserve to live an abundant life. You mean the world to Him, and He loves you to heaven and back.

Your value is beyond racial prejudices, cultural clichés, religious taboos, worldly paradigms, and social norms. Jesus broke all the walls so you can live in liberty. It's time for you to rise up and face the world with God-confidence. If the world points out the flaws, then point the world to Jesus, who is the epitome of perfection. You're worth every hail and every hurrah because you are His glorious masterpiece!

My beautiful sisters in Christ, whoever you are, whichever background you emerge from, and whatever you do, just know that you're totally worth it! Say it loud and say it again!

YOU ARE
HIS GLORIOUS
masterpiece

Chapter 2:
You Belong

How many of you have been in places where you've felt like you've never belonged? I've felt that way many, many times! The ambiguity and uncertainty in our journeys wear us out and disrupt our inner peace because we really can't perceive how things will end up or really can't tell if we're heading in the right direction. When we don't have all the answers, we immediately conclude that we're failing, and our lives are miserable.

Sometimes we feel as if the valleys we're walking in are becoming deeper and deeper as we walk. We feel like we're trapped and can never come out of them. But what we don't seem to notice is the presence of Jesus in all those valleys. There is no place we're going that Jesus has not already been, so why not allow Him to take over and help us overcome?

MY FRAME WAS NOT HIDDEN
FROM YOU WHEN I WAS MADE
IN THE SECRET PLACE...

PSALM 139:15, NIV

We as Christians sometimes try to cover things up and behave as if everything's okay, even in front of God. We really don't have to live like those people who cover up; we can instead can be the ones who uncover the deepest of thoughts in front of Him. How can we hide anything from Him? Even our very frame was not hidden from Him. So, by hiding our emotions, we're only hindering the intervention of His grace.

It's okay to say "it's not okay" in front of God. Don't deal with your struggles yourself. Let God deal with them because He never detests; He only delivers. When you look upon the cross, you will know where you belong. You don't just belong to His kingdom but also *His heart*.

> "THUS THE LORD HAS DEALT
> WITH ME, IN THE DAYS WHEN
> HE LOOKED ON ME, TO TAKE
> AWAY MY REPROACH AMONG PEOPLE."
>
> LUKE 1:25, NKJV

God will never let you go through something that doesn't end up working for your own good. All these trials are stepping-stones for elevated blessings! God can take even our wrong choices and hasty decisions and turn them into blessings in the end. So don't ever worry about the bad decisions you've made or the failures you've experienced. God is not going to invalidate you for those. He will accept you as you are and will still love you very much!

FOR EVERYONE WHO HAS
BEEN BORN OF GOD OVERCOMES THE
WORLD. AND THIS IS THE
VICTORY THAT HAS OVERCOME
THE WORLD—OUR FAITH. WHO IS IT THAT
OVERCOMES THE WORLD EXCEPT THE
ONE WHO BELIEVES THAT
JESUS IS THE SON OF GOD?

1 JOHN 5:4–5, ESV

Our lives are works in progress; experiencing His magnificent grace, even in the littlest of things, in every moment is a beautiful journey in itself. Our lives are like those beautiful paintings that start off with a dot or a line and don't look like anything recognizable in the beginning but at the end come together to form stunning works of art. The world is like a plain canvas, and our God, who is the best artist, is painting our pictures right now. Just imagine how beautifully He is going to paint the best of us on that canvas.

You're here for a reason, and God wants you to know that you belong! Talking about feeling out of place gives us a chance to ponder the life of a woman in the Bible who, even though she felt out of place many times, never gave up on God. It's the story of Queen Esther, born humbly but blessed supernaturally. When we read her story (Esther 2: 5-10), we see that she is taken into the palace of a Persian king, along with several other Persian women, as a candidate for queen. Since she couldn't reveal her identity as a Jew, she must have suffered a severe identity crisis from the time she stepped into the palace. Furthermore she must have also felt out of place, as she was not used to Persian culture and traditions. Despite the unfamiliarity she had to adapt to the Persian lifestyle pretty quickly.

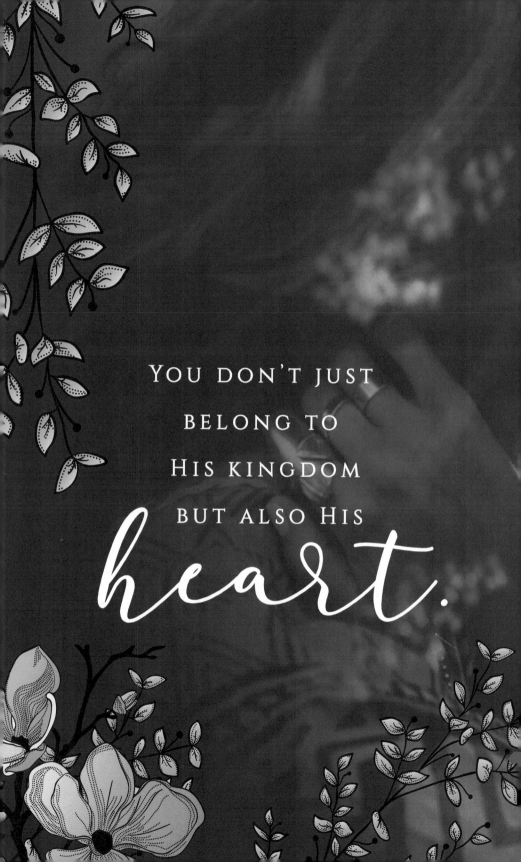

YOU DON'T JUST
BELONG TO
HIS KINGDOM
BUT ALSO HIS
heart.

NOW THE YOUNG WOMAN
PLEASED HIM, AND SHE
OBTAINED HIS FAVOR; SO HE READILY
GAVE BEAUTY PREPARATIONS TO HER,
BESIDES HER ALLOWANCE.
THEN SEVEN CHOICE MAIDSERVANTS
WERE PROVIDED FOR HER FROM THE
KING'S PALACE, AND HE MOVED
HER AND HER MAIDSERVANTS TO
THE BEST PLACE IN THE
HOUSE OF THE WOMEN.

ESTHER 2:9, NKJV

In the verse preceding this one, we read of a truly supernatural event. God's intention was never to leave Esther hanging in fear; that's why He quickly turned things around and gave her favor not just with anyone but with the custodian himself. What could she have done to obtain such favor and mercy? Absolutely nothing. It was the Lord who poured out His grace upon her only to make her realize that *He's right there with her* in every step of her way and she's not alone in this. The Lord made sure that she belonged in the palace! How many of us are afraid to take a step of faith, to do what the Lord is asking us to do because it may seem difficult? Can we take that step of faith and trust God to take care of us, just like Esther did? God is reminding us today that "it's going to be all right" and His grace is enough in all our *goings!*

Sometimes we might end up in situations that are uncomfortable, unrewarding, and unexpected, but God will never put us in places where His grace does not flow. He will, in no time, *elevate* us and put us in the *best* places because we are, alongside Esther, His chosen daughters. Esther was in the right place, but God moved her to the best place because that's where she truly belonged. Similarly we're meant to be not only in the right places but also the *best places* in life.

If we read further, we find that Esther was presented before the king after months of preparation. God always makes us go through a *process* before we receive our blessing because He prepares us for what lies *beyond the blessing*—His *purpose*. There was a season, an appointed time, for presenting Esther before the king. She was presented in the tenth month, which is the month of *Tebeth* according to the Hebrew calendar. The word *Tebeth* in Hebrew means "goodness." Just as Esther was presented in the season of the Lord's goodness, we as His children are actually living in the season of His goodness every single day. For Esther this season must have been like a test of time. But for God it was the perfect season of goodness.

Esther waited patiently all those months, not worrying about the outcome. She never felt the need to be competitive with others or show off her beauty because she knew in her heart that it wasn't worth fighting, only knowing that she was God's own. It must have been very hard for her to blend in, but she didn't give up and made an effort to conform. Although God did give her His favor, she had to play her part, to remain in the palace and allow Him to work in and through her.

THE KING LOVED ESTHER MORE
THAN ALL THE OTHER WOMEN,
AND SHE OBTAINED GRACE
AND FAVOR IN HIS SIGHT
MORE THAN ALL THE VIRGINS;
SO HE SET THE ROYAL CROWN
UPON HER HEAD AND MADE HER
QUEEN INSTEAD OF VASHTI.

ESTHER 2:17, NKJV

Don't retaliate against the world; remain in the Lord. The place of Esther is our place too—a place of waiting, trusting, submitting, and being content. Just as Esther was highly favored, deeply loved, greatly blessed, and received her royal crown, we as His "grace daughters" have already received our royal crowns by believing in the finished work of Jesus Christ. And, as He freely gives His grace, goodness, mercy, favor, love, joy, and peace, let us also freely receive without disbelief.

Esther becoming queen was not the end of the story. It was the beginning of something much greater. God prepared Esther for a *purpose that was beyond the blessing!* If we read further in the book of Esther (chapters 3 and 4), we see that Haman conspires against all the Jews in town and deceptively obtains the decree from the king to destroy them. When the news reaches Esther, she panics and dreads the potential danger of seeking an audience with the king, but God reminds Esther through Mordecai that she was called forth for such a time as this.

AND MORDECAI TOLD THEM TO
ANSWER ESTHER: "...YET WHO
KNOWS WHETHER YOU HAVE
COME TO THE KINGDOM FOR
SUCH A TIME AS THIS?"
THEN ESTHER TOLD THEM TO
REPLY TO MORDECAI:
"GO, GATHER ALL THE JEWS
WHO ARE PRESENT IN SHUSHAN,
AND FAST FOR ME; NEITHER EAT
NOR DRINK FOR THREE DAYS,
NIGHT OR DAY. MY MAIDS AND
I WILL FAST LIKEWISE. AND
SO I WILL GO TO THE KING,
WHICH IS AGAINST THE LAW;
AND IF I PERISH, I PERISH!"

ESTHER 4:13–16, NKJV

God can use anyone, anywhere. We're all aligned with His divine purpose, just like Esther. Sometimes when we get comfortable in our blessing, God reminds us that there is a purpose that lies beyond it. Esther was not only meant to be the Persian queen but also be the channel that God could use to save all the Jews. And what she did was truly commendable—she indeed responded to her calling and sought an audience with the king.

Although it was frightful and intense, Esther trusted the Lord and sought His wisdom to save the Jews! It was a matter of many lives that were at stake, but she didn't back out because she knew that God was with her. She didn't despise the power of God and thus carry out her own plan; instead she sought His favor and wisdom. Sometimes change can look a little different from what we picture in our minds, but if we embrace the change and accept the challenge, God will ensure our success. He is not a God of uncertainty but rather a God of clarity, precision, and perfection.

SO IT WAS, WHEN THE KING
SAW QUEEN ESTHER STANDING
IN THE COURT, THAT SHE FOUND FAVOR
IN HIS SIGHT, AND THE KING
HELD OUT TO ESTHER THE
GOLDEN SCEPTER THAT WAS IN
HIS HAND. THEN ESTHER WENT
NEAR AND TOUCHED THE TOP OF
THE SCEPTER. AND THE KING
SAID TO HER, "WHAT DO YOU
WISH, QUEEN ESTHER? WHAT
IS YOUR REQUEST? IT SHALL BE
GIVEN TO YOU—UP TO
HALF THE KINGDOM!"

ESTHER 5:2–3, NKJV

When the king saw her standing in the court, Esther found favor in his sight. Whoa! The response to her faith was favor and blessings! See how the Lord elevated Esther? Similarly, when we respond to God's calling, step out in faith, and stand in the place of His purpose, He will grant to us unprecedented favor and blessings.

Only if we truly believe that by trusting God our lives will turn out in the best possible way will we guarantee this outcome. It's hard to know what's in store for us, but it's easy to believe that something good must be in store. Isn't it? Sometimes it's those unknown places that become the most established places, and if we choose to step into them, He will make sure that we grow and prosper. Whatever is laid in front of you, whether it's a decision or a piece of advice, go to the Lord first, and He will give you an answer through His spirit, His Word, people, or a change in situation.

This whole story speaks of one thing—God's favor being on Esther because she was chosen for His purpose. She, on the other hand, chose to be content in the middle of a challenge and not give up. Similarly when we truly believe that there is something beyond our blessing, we can allow our hearts belong to the "*now*" place of His purpose.

Otherwise we will be in a constant state of delusion and fear about tomorrow. Our lives are not a compromise. Jesus will turn every situation in our favor so that we may live content. Often times we are disappointed because our lives seem different than what we envisioned.

Many times we think of contentment as some sort of a "happy state," where life runs pretty smoothly and steadily without any disruptions. But this is what God taught me about contentment: *"Contentment is not a state; it's a posture."* It's a posture of faith that we take, trusting Him when situations make us weary, when life is tough, when we don't have all the answers, or when we don't have it all sorted out. When we rely on God, no matter where we are, assured that He will give us what we need, we can truly be content. He's reminding us that it's gonna be okay! Even if the mountain we're climbing seems too high or the valley we're walking through seems too deep, *we will make it to the other side.*

Esther was able to be content despite the unanswered questions, uncertainties, and ambiguity surrounding her because she knew that God would figure it out for her. She took the posture of faith and relied on Him completely. She didn't run away but remained in the palace and faced the situation. God is reminding you too to stay in those places of obscurity, even if nothing makes sense. Don't run away but remain and trust, just like Esther did, that He will reorient you—wait, pray, step forward in faith, and stand! Do what you're asked to do, and He will do what's best for you!

NOW GOD HAS US WHERE HE WANTS US,
WITH ALL THE TIME IN THIS WORLD
AND THE NEXT TO SHOWER GRACE
AND KINDNESS UPON US IN
CHRIST JESUS. SAVING IS ALL HIS IDEA,
AND ALL HIS WORK. ALL WE DO IS TRUST
HIM ENOUGH TO LET HIM DO IT.
IT'S GOD'S GIFT FROM START TO FINISH!
WE DON'T PLAY THE MAJOR ROLE.
IF WE DID, WE'D PROBABLY GO AROUND
BRAGGING THAT WE'D DONE THE WHOLE
THING! NO, WE NEITHER MAKE NOR SAVE
OURSELVES. GOD DOES BOTH THE MAKING
AND SAVING. HE CREATES EACH OF US BY
CHRIST JESUS TO JOIN HIM IN
THE WORK HE DOES, THE GOOD WORK
HE HAS GOTTEN READY FOR US TO DO,
WORK WE HAD BETTER BE DOING.

EPHESIANS 2:7–10, MSG

Just as the verse states, God has us where He wants us, so let's stop thinking that we're in the wrong place. We're indeed in the right place, so let's stop doubting the place of His purpose. Did Esther ever plan to be in the palace for that long? No! Did she prepare herself for this new endeavor? No! Did she know anything about the process or the outcome? No! And, even though she didn't have a clue about anything, she still chose to step into the place chosen by God because she was convinced in her heart that He would prepare her, take care of her, provide for her, and also make her belong.

If you're in a place like Esther's, don't try to leave; stay because you are meant to be in that place for God's good work. He's about to do something great in and through you, and He's in that place with you, so He will make sure you shine, you rise, you belong, you're blessed, and that you'll be a blessing! The world might make you feel left out, but you're actually *left in* for a *blessing*!

MEANWHILE, THE MOMENT
WE GET TIRED IN THE WAITING,
GOD'S SPIRIT IS RIGHT ALONGSIDE
HELPING US ALONG. IF WE DON'T
KNOW HOW OR WHAT TO PRAY,
IT DOESN'T MATTER. HE DOES OUR
PRAYING IN AND FOR US,
MAKING PRAYER OUT OF OUR
WORDLESS SIGHS, OUR ACHING GROANS.
HE KNOWS US FAR BETTER THAN WE
KNOW OURSELVES, KNOWS OUR
PREGNANT CONDITION, AND KEEPS US
PRESENT BEFORE GOD. THAT'S WHY
WE CAN BE SO SURE THAT EVERY
DETAIL IN OUR LIVES OF LOVE FOR GOD IS
WORKED INTO SOMETHING GOOD.

ROMANS 8:26-28, MSG

THE WORLD MIGHT
MAKE YOU FEEL LEFT OUT,
BUT YOU'RE ACTUALLY
LEFT IN FOR A
blessing!

Chapter 3:
A-Game
Not Needed

Amid the world we're living in, each one of us invariably wants to bring our A-game to the table because we want to prove that we won't settle for anything other than the best. We will even sacrifice everything in order to make it big. It's not only about how far we have made it but also about how successful and recognized we are. We measure our success by social status, wealth, and—in this millennial generation—by the number of followers we have on social media. Our lives have become open books; everyone knows everything about everyone else because the details are out in the open. Knowingly or unknowingly, we've become dependent on people's opinions in making choices and sometimes even accepting ourselves. The problem here is not working but pushing hard to overachieve. As believers, we're stuck in two parallel worlds, one based on "work your way through it" and another based on "Jesus already worked it out." Which world are we living in?

THE LORD WILL PERFECT THAT WHICH CONCERNS ME...

PSALM 138:8, NKJV

Can we comprehend the perfection of our God, who created the sun, placed those sparkling stars in the sky, formed all the planets and beyond? We absolutely cannot! Then won't He perfect everything that concerns us? Of course, He will! Our job is not to fix things but to fixate on He who is able to give us exceedingly, abundantly, above all that we ask for or think of (refer to Ephesians 3:20). This doesn't mean we get to laze around; it simply means that in the work we do, we don't have to stress out and panic. Instead, rely on Him. As women, we have a whirlwind of thoughts circling our minds every single moment, whether household chores such as cleaning, cooking, planning groceries, prepping food, doing dishes, and laundry or our personal interests such as shopping, catching up with friends, and the like. Our minds are programmed to process many things at one time, but sometimes carrying the burden of "planning things" is overwhelming. We easily get frustrated when things don't work out according to our plans. Sometimes life doesn't happen according to our plans, and that's okay. It's good to plan, but it's not good to get disappointed if plans don't work out. God wants us to give ourselves some grace. He is in control of our lives and we can rest only if we trust. So everyday let's take a break, sit for a moment, breathe in, and allow Him to minister. We need that "God-time" in order to rejuvenate, refresh and restfully get back to life.

IT IS VAIN FOR YOU TO RISE
EARLY, TO RETIRE LATE, TO
EAT THE BREAD OF ANXIOUS
LABORS—FOR HE GIVES
[BLESSINGS] TO HIS BELOVED
EVEN IN HIS SLEEP.

PSALM 127:2, AMP

Just as the verse says, even when we're sleeping, God is continually blessing. Our God is a good God; He never withholds but always outpours.

God reminded me of Ruth's story when He gave me the title for this chapter. Ruth, after her husband's passing, chose to go with her mother-in-law, Naomi, to Bethlehem, hoping for a better life. Ruth was a moabite, but she accepted the God of Israel, made Him her God, and completely trusted Him to create a better future for her. Although she had the option to go back and live with her parents, she chose to go where the Lord led her. That really got me thinking about her heart of humility, faith, and grace.

BUT RUTH SAID: "ENTREAT ME NOT TO LEAVE YOU, OR TO TURN BACK FROM FOLLOWING AFTER YOU; FOR WHEREVER YOU GO, I WILL GO; AND WHEREVER YOU LODGE, I WILL LODGE; YOUR PEOPLE SHALL BE MY PEOPLE, AND YOUR GOD, MY GOD."

RUTH 1:16, NKJV

Sometimes, it's not just our works but also our attitude toward them that determines our faith. It's not about what we do; it's about the faith we carry when we act. It's about placing our expectations solely on the Lord and believing that He will always work all things together for our own *good,* and that *with Him nothing can go wrong.*

AND RUTH THE MOABITE SAID TO NAOMI, "LET ME GO TO THE FIELDS AND PICK UP THE LEFTOVER GRAIN BEHIND ANYONE IN WHOSE EYES I FIND FAVOR." NAOMI SAID TO HER, "GO AHEAD, MY DAUGHTER."

RUTH 2:2, NIV

Although Ruth was in a somewhat hopeless situation, not knowing what her future held, she was expectant of good things and continued serving Naomi. After they settled down in Bethlehem, Ruth went out to a field one day to glean so she could gather some grain for herself and her mother-in-law. She was completely unaware of the fact that the field she chose to work in belonged to one of their relatives, Boaz. Well, can we believe that God puts us in the *right place at the right time?*

Ruth went in with no expectations, no A-game whatsoever. It's not as if she took training classes on how to glean. She just went with a humble heart. That's all it takes—a heart that says, *"Yes, Lord, I will go where you'll take me."* Ruth wanted to pick up the leftover grain behind anyone in whose eyes she found favor, but when she went to the field, she found favor with not just anyone but the owner of the field. God turned things around in Ruth's favor and surprised her.

When Boaz entered the field, he inquired about Ruth's identity and learned that she was Naomi's daughter-in-law. He then asked Ruth to stay in his field and continue gleaning and also gave her permission to drink from the water jars whenever she was thirsty (Ruth 2: 8-9). Isn't it amazing to see how God planned things ahead? He made her feel special by giving her attention. He didn't let anyone treat Ruth like a nobody and instead granted her special favor.

AT THIS, SHE BOWED DOWN
WITH HER FACE TO THE
GROUND. SHE ASKED HIM,
"WHY HAVE I FOUND SUCH
FAVOR IN YOUR EYES THAT YOU
NOTICE ME—A FOREIGNER?"

RUTH 2:10, NIV

Yes, Lord!

I WILL GO WHERE
YOU'LL TAKE ME.

Ruth was startled by Boaz's gesture. Being a foreigner, she never expected such a response from the owner, but little did she know how much God valued her. It wasn't her skill that gave her the blessing but rather her heart, which said "yes" to God. And of course He will change times and seasons because she's chosen by Him.

Sometimes, when we're in such foreign places, we tend to carry a "stranger mentality." We struggle to adjust in the current season because we keep thinking about what might happen next. Even though Ruth was apprehensive and nervous, she didn't refrain from what she was supposed to do in that season, which was work in the fields and help out. She carried out her role as a gleaner, not worrying about whether she would thrive, get paid enough, or be promoted. Her thoughts were in the current season, the one in which God had placed her, and not in the next. Oftentimes we struggle in the current season because our thoughts are not in the current but the next.

BOAZ REPLIED, "I'VE BEEN TOLD ALL ABOUT WHAT YOU HAVE DONE FOR YOUR MOTHER-IN-LAW SINCE THE DEATH OF YOUR HUSBAND—HOW YOU LEFT YOUR FATHER AND MOTHER AND YOUR HOMELAND AND CAME TO LIVE WITH A PEOPLE YOU DID NOT KNOW BEFORE. MAY THE LORD REPAY YOU FOR WHAT YOU HAVE DONE. MAY YOU BE RICHLY REWARDED BY THE LORD, THE GOD OF ISRAEL, UNDER WHOSE WINGS YOU HAVE COME TO TAKE REFUGE."

RUTH 2:11-12, NIV

Ruth never wished for any sort of validation from anyone for her service, but isn't it amazing to see the way God valued her service and honored her in front of Boaz? It's the Lord who repays us, and not the people. We don't have to impress people to get noticed; we need to confide in God and own our portion, just like Ruth did. Don't judge yourself based on the position you're in right now. It might seem insignificant, but it doesn't make you incapable of success. God is your very present help in time of need.

When we seek the Lord in every little step we take, *we will not only get the blessing but will also be the blessing.* We will serve others out of the abundance we receive from Him. The following verse reiterates God's loving kindness and mercy toward His beloved daughter.

AND WHEN SHE ROSE UP TO
GLEAN, BOAZ COMMANDED
HIS YOUNG MEN, SAYING, "LET HER
GLEAN EVEN AMONG THE SHEAVES,
AND DO NOT REPROACH HER.
ALSO LET GRAIN FROM THE
BUNDLES FALL PURPOSELY
FOR HER; LEAVE IT THAT SHE
MAY GLEAN, AND DO NOT
REBUKE HER."

RUTH 2:15–16, NKJV

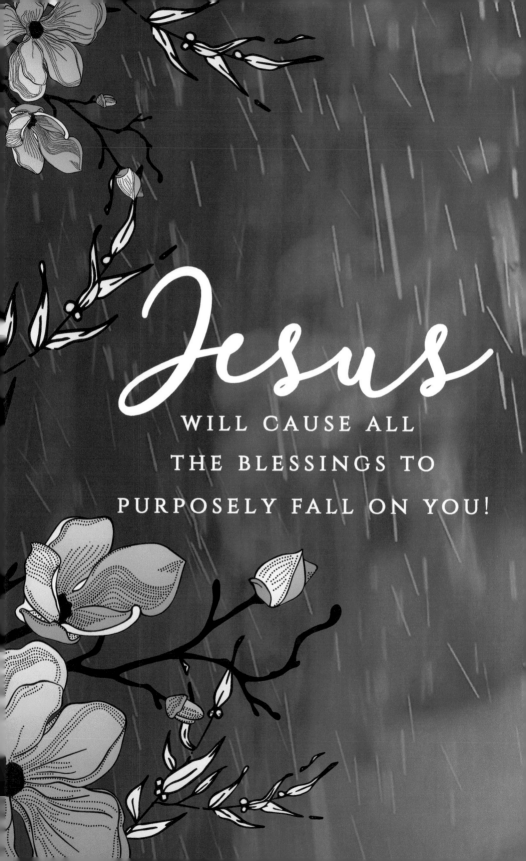

Jesus

WILL CAUSE ALL
THE BLESSINGS TO
PURPOSELY FALL ON YOU!

Ruth had planned to pick up grain from among the leftovers, but God gave her the finest grain from the sheaves. Even when she had no expectations, the Lord blessed her. As Ruth's story implies, the Lord will cause all the blessings to *purposely* fall on us. When we're in a hopeless situation, the Lord will open a door of blessing that no one can shut. No A-game needed whatsoever. Jesus purposed us to receive His grace upon grace for every need, so let's stop striving and start receiving.

THE BLESSING OF THE LORD MAKES A PERSON RICH, AND HE ADDS NO SORROW WITH IT.

PROVERBS 10:22, NLT

The best part is that there's no reproach, rebuke, or sorrow in the Lord's blessing. Don't we serve a loving God, who stretches forth His hands only to bless us? Let us be overjoyed knowing that Jesus qualified all of us for His extraordinary grace, and it's not what we do but whom we belong to that matters the most in life.

Jesus is so very beautiful and amazing in every way! Just remember that He loves you very much, and He will cause all the blessings to purposely fall on you just to see you smile!

HE WILL ONCE AGAIN FILL YOUR MOUTH WITH LAUGHTER AND YOUR LIPS WITH SHOUTS OF JOY.

JOB 8:21, NLT

God is watching over you; He will bring a shift in your life. He will never overlook but will meet every need of yours. Jesus is the only A-game you will ever need to bring to the table! That's all it takes to overcome any situation in life. He is working in your favor right now, so get ready to see things change!

Chapter 4:
RE-START

All of us go through seasons of dryness and inadequacy—"seasons of famine"—wherein we feel like nothing's working out and no one understands us. Even I went through such a season not long ago, during which I felt like my whole world was a void and my head was filled with empty thoughts. I felt emotionally burdened by the weight of negative circumstances, condemnation, and disappointment. I was fearful to talk to anyone because I thought that I was totally worthless and unwanted. I started accepting the lies, sought constant validation, and slowly slipped into a world of disbelief as I started to judge myself. I knew I was drowning in delusional fears and fabricated whispers. I was in a thought loop that never ended, and I didn't feel like seeking the Lord because I was very weak in spirit.

One afternoon I called my brother just to talk casually, but the Lord led me to share my situation. After hearing the situation, he said, "You know something? With Jesus, you can always restart your life." That line encouraged me so much. It was as if a wave of peace had just come upon me after I was reminded that, yes, Jesus was with me, that there would always be a restart to my life, and that I didn't have to be stuck in such a season anymore. After the call I sat on the couch thinking about that line and, suddenly, the image of Jesus hanging on the cross appeared in front of my eyes. I heard Him say,

"You're my beloved daughter, in whom I am well pleased." Tears started rolling down my face, and I instantly felt loved and cared for. I felt like Jesus understood my feelings even though the whole world didn't even care to listen.

Sometimes a simple reminder about Jesus can restore the lost peace in our lives, and that's what I experienced that day. It's so important to pause and remind ourselves of the Lord's amazing grace! That's the only constant in our lives. He could have died for anything else, but He chose us over everything else and considered each one of us worthy of His precious sacrifice. Even when He breathed His final breath, He only thought about you and me. He didn't back off but went all the way, and overcame the world just for us, making us completely blameless. So only He has the final say over our lives. Let us acknowledge His love, leave behind yesterday's story, and restart today with Jesus.

> WHAT MARVELOUS LOVE THE
> FATHER HAS EXTENDED TO US!
> JUST LOOK AT IT—WE'RE
> CALLED CHILDREN OF GOD!
> THAT'S WHO WE REALLY ARE...
>
> 1 JOHN 3:1, MSG

God gave us access to heavenly riches, and He's interested in restoring and assuring that we prosper in every area of our lives, be it physical, spiritual, or emotional. Don't give up on Jesus yet! Hold on to Him. He is the eternal source of blessings to all His children! Stop settling for the bare minimum! Dream big and never give up.

AND MY GOD WILL LIBERALLY SUPPLY (FILL UNTIL FULL) YOUR EVERY NEED ACCORDING TO HIS RICHES IN GLORY IN CHRIST JESUS.

PHILIPPIANS 4:19, AMP

There are many stories in the Bible of people's lives undergoing an amazing restart, but the Lord reminded me of one in particular—the very beautiful restoration story of the Shunammite woman in 2 Kings 4:8–37 and 2 Kings 8:1–6. This woman has been barren for a long time, her husband is elderly, and there is no hope left of her having a child. When the prophet Elisha visits her town, she persuades him to eat and stay in her house because she knows that Elisha is a man of God and that he will definitely pray and intercede for her.

God may use any means to speak to us and bring blessings upon us. All we gotta do is lean into His will and be led by His spirit always. This must be our motto: "Not mine, but thy will be done in my life." The next day, Elisha learns that the woman doesn't have a child, so he gives her a word of promise that she will have a child by next year.

> ...AND SHE SAID, "NO, MY LORD. MAN OF GOD, DO NOT LIE TO YOUR MAIDSERVANT!" BUT THE WOMAN CONCEIVED, AND BORE A SON WHEN THE APPOINTED TIME HAD COME, OF WHICH ELISHA HAD TOLD HER.
>
> 2 KINGS 4:16–17, NKJV

Even after Elisha gives her the promise, she refuses to believe and immediately says "no." Nevertheless, the woman conceives at the appointed time. Her "no" has no effect on God's "yes." Even when we disregard, our good God never disappoints. He's faithful even to the faithless. Just know that your promise in on the way! So be hopeful, it's worth the wait.

"I DON'T THINK THE WAY YOU THINK.
THE WAY YOU WORK ISN'T THE WAY
I WORK." GOD'S DECREE. "FOR AS THE SKY
SOARS HIGH ABOVE EARTH, SO THE
WAY I WORK SURPASSES THE WAY
YOU WORK, AND THE WAY I THINK
IS BEYOND THE WAY YOU THINK.
JUST AS RAIN AND SNOW DESCEND
FROM THE SKIES AND DON'T GO BACK
UNTIL THEY'VE WATERED THE EARTH,
DOING THEIR WORK OF MAKING
THINGS GROW AND BLOSSOM,
PRODUCING SEED FOR FARMERS
AND FOOD FOR THE HUNGRY, SO
WILL THE WORDS THAT COME OUT
OF MY MOUTH NOT COME BACK
EMPTY-HANDED. THEY'LL DO THE
WORK I SENT THEM TO DO,
THEY'LL COMPLETE THE
ASSIGNMENT I GAVE THEM.

ISAIAH 55:8–11, MSG

Even after the Shunammite woman doubted, the promise still came to pass at the "appointed time" of the Lord. Our doubts cannot stop His promises from being fulfilled. As the verse I just quoted says, God doesn't think the way we think. He doesn't move according to our plans, and His words never return empty but rather complete the assignment. So rest assured that God is working!

As women, we emotionally break down if things go haywire and, therefore, fight our battles with tears because we reason with our hearts. Don't we? But, all our tear drops are reaching God's feet and He's keeping a count of all of them because they're very precious to Him. He knows what we're going through, and it hurts Him to see us in distress. He will not let us stay in those seasons of drought for long. So, even if it's tough, let us hold our peace and not react with anger but respond with faith!

YOU'VE KEPT TRACK OF MY EVERY TOSS AND TURN THROUGH THE SLEEPLESS NIGHTS, EACH TEAR ENTERED IN YOUR LEDGER, EACH ACHE WRITTEN IN YOUR BOOK.

PSALM 56:8, MSG

God even keeps track of our long sleepless nights. It's fruitless to stress out about things that are not in our control. By losing sleep we're not going to win over the worry. It's simply adding another level of stress on top of the existing one. It's time to change the way we respond. We shouldn't let our concerns corner us and keep us isolated. We can still carry joy, even when everything around seems dark and gloomy. Our faith will triumph because we hoped in the Lord. So let's keep that faith going! Let's see how the Shunammite woman responded to one of the biggest battles of her life.

AND THE CHILD GREW. NOW IT HAPPENED ONE DAY THAT HE WENT OUT TO THIS FATHER, TO THE REAPERS. AND HE SAID TO HIS FATHER, "MY HEAD, MY HEAD!"...WHEN HE HAD TAKEN HIM AND BROUGHT HIM TO HIS MOTHER, HE SAT ON HER KNEES TILL NOON, AND THEN DIED...THEN SHE CALLED TO HER HUSBAND, AND SAID, "PLEASE SEND ME ONE OF THE YOUNG MEN AND ONE OF THE DONKEYS, THAT I MAY RUN TO THE MAN OF GOD AND COME BACK." SO HE SAID, "WHY ARE YOU GOING TO HIM TODAY? IT IS NEITHER THE NEW MOON NOR THE SABBATH." AND SHE SAID, "IT IS WELL." THEN SHE SADDLED

A DONKEY, AND SAID TO HER SERVANT, "DRIVE, AND GO FORWARD; DO NOT SLACKEN THE PACE FOR ME UNLESS I TELL YOU."

2 KINGS 4:18-24, NKJV

Even when the woman loses her precious child, she doesn't give up on God and start grieving, instead trusting Him to deliver a miracle. She decides to visit Elisha in hopeful anticipation. On the way out, when her husband questions her, she responds, saying *"it is well"* and went ahead to meet the man of God. The most beautiful part of the story comes when she decides to go forward and not look back. She believes that there is more to her life and refuses to be stuck in grief. She is convinced that no matter what happens in life, it is well with her soul. Her faith pushes her to be hopeful.

Many times we're stuck in the same seasons of grief because we keep looking back and thinking about what we have lost rather than focusing on the new beginnings with Jesus. When we face those hopeless moments in life, and when people keep disappointing us with doubts, are we ready to say "it is well" and run to God instead of fostering those negative thoughts and letting them become our reality? Let us hold fast to our faith and go forward to that place of grace where we'll find our help.

It is well
with my
soul

The Lord eventually helped the woman by sending Elisha to her house to restore the boy's life. Similarly, the Lord never disappoints us when we go to Him despite the odds. The woman saw the biggest miracle of her life, but the Lord was not done with her yet! If we read further in 2 Kings 8:1-6, we see that the woman, along with her family, goes to live in the land of the Philistines for seven years because Elisha advises her of the forthcoming famine in her land. She immediately follows his instructions and relocates to this new place. It is amazing to see the Lord rescue her even before the famine hits her. He is already in control of her impending situation. In the same way, God wants us to remember that *when famine hits us, His grace hits us harder!* All we have to do is prepare ourselves to go where the Lord is willing to take us!

The woman had to restart her life in this new land with new people, but she did it without a doubt because she knew that with God on her side all would be well! Similarly when we're hit with the toughest, driest situations, shall we not dwell in the worry but walk into His presence? God is reminding us to leave behind the land of famine and enter into the land of promise, just like the woman did.

WHY IS EVERYONE HUNGRY FOR MORE? "MORE, MORE," THEY SAY. "MORE, MORE." I HAVE GOD'S MORE-THAN ENOUGH, MORE JOY IN ONE ORDINARY DAY THAN THEY GET IN ALL THEIR SHOPPING SPREES. AT DAY'S END I'M READY FOR SOUND SLEEP, FOR YOU, GOD, HAVE PUT MY LIFE BACK TOGETHER.

PSALM 4:6–8, MSG

Our God is not a God of just enough but a God of more than enough! Our acceptance of His grace is the true source of our strength when we're weak. If we read further in 2 Kings 8:3-5, we see that the woman goes back to her land after the famine ends. Later she visits the king's court to appeal for her house and land. In the meantime the king asks Gehazi to share the great things Elisha has done. So Gehazi shares the testimony of the Shunammite woman's son, whose life was restored, and it so happens that the woman is present in the king's court while he shares her story. God took her to the court at the right time. His timing is perfect!

WHEN FAMINE HITS US,
HIS *grace* HITS
US HARDER!

AND WHEN THE KING
ASKED THE WOMAN, SHE TOLD HIM.
SO THE KING APPOINTED A CERTAIN
OFFICER FOR HER, SAYING, "RESTORE
ALL THAT WAS HERS, AND ALL THE
PROCEEDS OF THE FIELD FROM THE
DAY THAT SHE LEFT THE LAND
UNTIL NOW."

2 KINGS 8:6, NKJV

The woman just went up there with her petition like any other ordinary woman, but God granted her extraordinary grace. And, of course, restored not just a day's worth of what she had lost but everything that ever belonged to her. What a great ending to the story! Similarly God is writing each one of our stories so perfectly that there's absolutely no room for incompleteness. Just keep propelling forward according to His momentum, and He will restore everything we have lost and much more!

> "SO I WILL RESTORE TO
> YOU THE YEARS THAT THE
> SWARMING LOCUST HAS EATEN,
> THE CRAWLING LOCUST, THE
> CONSUMING LOCUST, AND
> THE CHEWING LOCUST, MY
> GREAT ARMY WHICH I SENT AMONG
> YOU. YOU SHALL EAT IN PLENTY AND
> BE SATISFIED, AND PRAISE THE NAME OF
> THE LORD YOUR GOD, WHO
> HAS DEALT WONDROUSLY WITH
> YOU; AND MY PEOPLE SHALL
> NEVER BE PUT TO SHAME."
>
> JOEL 2:25-26, NKJV

With Jesus, there's always a restart to our lives! If we truly believe that He can do it, He will do it! Don't live in the world of yesterday because that's not where you're meant to be. You just gotta move on! Don't miss out on the best season by being stuck in the past one. If we keep looking back, we will be distracted. Since God promised to restore everything, He will definetely restore, so let's stop worrying and overthinking.

NOW THAT WE KNOW
WHAT WE HAVE—JESUS, THIS GREAT
HIGH PRIEST WITH READY ACCESS TO
GOD—LET'S NOT LET IT SLIP
THROUGH OUR FINGERS. WE DON'T
HAVE A PRIEST WHO IS OUT OF
TOUCH WITH OUR REALITY. HE'S
BEEN THROUGH WEAKNESS
AND TESTING, EXPERIENCED
IT ALL—ALL BUT THE SIN.
SO LET'S WALK RIGHT UP TO
HIM AND GET WHAT HE IS SO READY
TO GIVE. TAKE THE MERCY,
ACCEPT THE HELP.

HEBREWS 4:16, MSG

Just as the verse says, we have a high priest who knows our reality. Don't ever think that He doesn't care or is unaware of our situation. He knows every detail of our lives and is willing to help us. But are we ready to accept His help? It's never too late to restart our lives with Jesus! Let us go boldly to Him to receive bountifully from Him!

Chapter 5:
SHE BELIEVED!

> ## BLESSED IS SHE WHO HAS BELIEVED THAT THE LORD WOULD FULFILL HIS PROMISES TO HER!
>
> ### LUKE 1:45, NIV

The Word of God says that we're already blessed when we believe in Jesus. Our blessings are directly proportional to our faith, not our works. We receive because we believe in Him. I used to always wonder whether huge blessings could come through my little faith, and sometimes I felt as if this were too good to be true until God started teaching me about faith. I learned that faith is not asking God to do what I want to do but rather allowing Him to do what He wills Himself to do!

Sometimes in life we end up in battles that are invisible and question our faith. These are harder to translate or express and oftentimes more tiring and exhausting than physical battles. The struggle seems real to us, but no one can either see it or understand the magnitude of it. We then end up embracing anonymity and isolation. Well, today Jesus wants to remind each of us that we don't have to fight those battles because He has already paid for all our emotional and mental struggles as well on that cross and called it "finished." And, if we allow Him to take over, He will free us from all those burdens.

We're not meant to live our lives in fear but rather in freedom. The world is a very dangerous place to invest our joy in. It will only disappoint and break us down because it's uncertain, fickle, and fleeting. Each one of our lives is more valuable than everything in this world combined. God didn't create us to just breathe and exist but to live happily, gloriously, and victoriously, enjoying His grace, goodness, and freedom every single day. Does the one breathing into us every second not know what we're struggling with daily? Of course He knows! He wants us to reach out to Him and accept His help. He's willing to give rest to our tired minds and comfort to our distressed souls. Are we willing to let Him do so?

One day, I was reading the story of the woman with the issue of blood from Mark 5. This story resonates with every woman struggling with those emotional fears. What's beautiful about this story is that it showcases both the woman's faith and the father's heart.

NOW A CERTAIN WOMAN HAD A FLOW OF BLOOD FOR TWELVE YEARS, AND HAD SUFFERED MANY THINGS FROM MANY PHYSICIANS. SHE HAD SPENT ALL THAT SHE HAD AND WAS NO BETTER, BUT RATHER GREW WORSE.

MARK 5:25-26, NKJV

We read in this passage that the woman suffered with the issue of blood for twelve years. That's a very long time to deal with something that's so painful. We all know what it feels like to have those extra long days of continuous bleeding and cramps. It feels just terrible! I can totally relate to this story because I struggled with polycystic ovary syndrome (PCOS) for many years, and I know what it feels like to go through those cycles of long periods. IIt takes a toll on both physical and emotional health. The woman in the Bible spent all that she had on treatments and doctor visits and still wasn't cured; her condition in fact worsened. Just imagine her emotional state each time she visited a doctor or underwent a treatment but yielded no positive results—she must have felt completely devastated and hopeless.

Waking up to the same old thing day after day is quite frustrating. And, because of her condition, she most likely had to live away from society and dreaded going out in public. She also fought those silent emotional battles for twelve long years. Her emotional problems likely became a common topic of discussion among those around her. And, because of that, she must have lived in condemnation and shame, unable to walk or talk freely. During those times she must have longed for someone who could really understand what she was going through.

At some point, though, she heard about Jesus and His miracles. Even though she had tried everything else and didn't see things change, she still decided to try Jesus because *she belived* that He could heal her. Disappointed but hopeful, she went to meet Him.

WHEN SHE HEARD ABOUT JESUS,
SHE CAME BEHIND HIM IN
THE CROWD AND TOUCHED
HIS GARMENT. FOR SHE SAID,
"IF ONLY I MAY TOUCH HIS CLOTHES,
I SHALL BE MADE WELL."

MARK 5:27–28, NKJV

The woman pushed herself through the crowds to get to Jesus. After she touched His garment, she believed and affirmed that she would be made well. And, immediately, she received her healing. Even though it was tough, her faith pushed her to go through the crowds. Sometimes *it's those places of discomfort that become the places of our miracle*. It's okay to step into those places because Jesus is already there, and He's allowing us to step into them only to heal us!

Many people surrounded Jesus, but the woman could see only him and no one else. She made her *miracle personal,* keeping it between her and Jesus. We have Jesus living in us, yet we make Him an outsider sometimes. Although He's so very near, we keep Him so far away.

IMMEDIATELY THE BLEEDING STOPPED,
AND SHE COULD FEEL IN HER BODY
THAT SHE HAD BEEN HEALED OF
HER TERRIBLE CONDITION...
BUT HE KEPT ON LOOKING AROUND
TO SEE WHO HAD DONE IT.
THEN THE FRIGHTENED WOMAN,
TREMBLING AT THE REALIZATION OF
WHAT HAD HAPPENED TO HER,
CAME AND FELL TO HER KNEES
IN FRONT OF HIM AND TOLD HIM
WHAT SHE HAD DONE. AND HE SAID
TO HER, "DAUGHTER, YOUR FAITH
HAS MADE YOU WELL. GO IN PEACE.
YOUR SUFFERING IS OVER."

MARK 5:29–34, NLT

Even though Jesus was physically far away from this woman, He was very near in her heart. Can we make Jesus personal? Can we go to Him even if there are many voices surrounding and stopping us from going? If only we could go to Him without fear, if only we could go to Him without being self-conscious, and if only we could reach out to Him, He will never disappoint us. The word faith in Greek is *pistis*, which translates literally to "firm persuasion." The woman persuaded Jesus like there was only one way she could be healed. She carried no doubt in her heart and strongly believed that only He had the power to heal her. The words "if only" not only demonstrated her faith but also the free access Jesus gave her to reach out to Him. He allowed her to come to Him without imposing any rules or restrictions and made His grace available without any conditions.

After Jesus realized the woman was healed, He kept searching for her. He didn't leave without showing the world how much she meant to Him. He also made her share her testimony in front of the crowd because He wanted everyone to know that her story was significant. And, by calling her "*daughter*," He valued her in front of everyone. All the years of pain must have vanished instantly, and she must have felt so happy and consoled. Such a beautiful sight! *Jesus never lets us be hidden; He always allows us to shine.* Jesus has time for each one of us and waits to hear, see, bless, and heal us.

BUT HIS DISCIPLES SAID TO HIM, "YOU SEE THE MULTITUDE THRONGING YOU, AND YOU SAY, 'WHO TOUCHED ME?'"

MARK 5:31, NKJV

The world considered this woman insignificant and unimportant. But Jesus stopped just for this one woman because He considered her precious, important, and worthy of all His attention. Even when the disciples didn't care to find out who had touched His robe, Jesus never gave up, but waited for her so that everyone could witness the beauty of the miracle. When the loud voices around us try to break us down, let's push ourselves to call out the name of Jesus because at the mention of His name every sickness is healed, every fear is silenced, and every chain is broken.

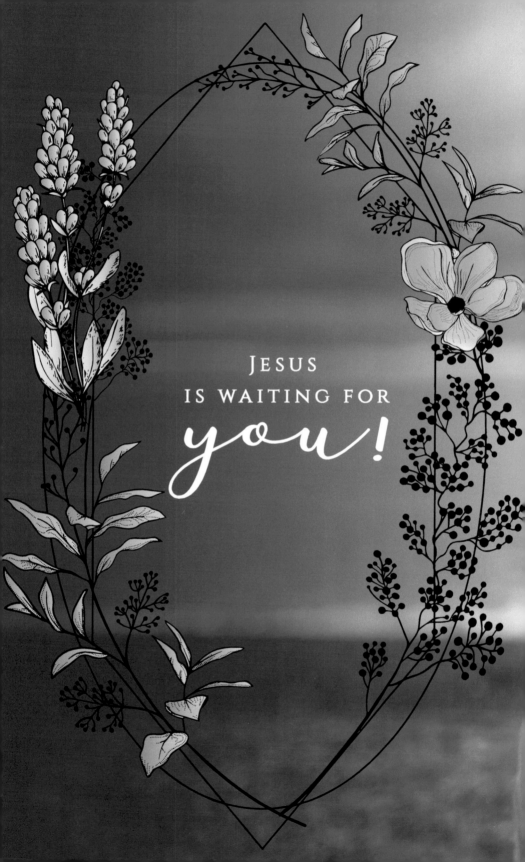

If we observe carefully, we see that the woman never went to Jesus for emotional healing. She only wanted to be healed of her physical condition, but He knew exactly what the woman needed even before she came to Him. He was fully aware of every detail of her suffering. If the woman were just physically healed, she would have still suffered from insecurity because she had lived in fear and denial all her life. So, by healing her from all her cares, He granted her freedom in every area. He also restored her confidence and identity by addressing her as "daughter" in front of everyone. He silenced the crowd so her voice could be heard. Her miracle was fully complete in Jesus!

AND HE SAID TO HER,
DAUGHTER, YOUR FAITH (YOUR
TRUST AND CONFIDENCE IN
ME, SPRINGING FROM FAITH
IN GOD) HAS RESTORED YOU
TO HEALTH. GO IN (INTO)
PEACE AND BE CONTINUALLY
HEALED AND FREED FROM YOUR
[DISTRESSING BODILY] DISEASE.

MARK 5:34, AMPC

I love the passage that states, "Go into peace and be continually healed and freed from your distressing disease." It's a promise of continued hope, peace, healing, and freedom. Jesus told the woman to step into the state of peace and be continually healed from physical illness and freed from emotional stress. In short, He made her whole. Wow! What a beautiful miracle! The woman could then enjoy both health and freedom. There's freedom in God's miracles. Even though the woman didn't ask for a breakthrough in every area, He still resorted every area of her life.

God considers every single issue concerning us, small or big, to be very important. Everything that concerns us, concerns Him, and He will never disregard any of our problems. He wants us to enjoy His goodness and live in His freedom. The woman's miracle is a beautiful depiction of the Father's love for His beloved daughter. His heart's content was to see His daughter not only healed but also *made whole*, completely restored, and fully satisfied!

Your prayer and His answer—nothing else matters. Don't become overwhelmed, my sisters. Don't be dismayed. *Our promise comes through the crowds and crowns us.* No one can stop it from happening! The woman came in fear but left in freedom! In the same way, when we go to Him despite our fears, failures, and insecurities, we will be set free.

> ## BUT YOU, LORD, ARE A SHIELD AROUND ME, MY GLORY, THE ONE WHO LIFTS MY HEAD HIGH.
>
> ### PSALM 3:3, NIV

The Lord is your shield, your glory, and the lifter of your head. You don't have to live for people or live by their opinions. God made room on this planet so you could live for His glory. Even if the world keeps blaming, know that it will not affect your blessing in anyway because *the boundary of your blessing is between you and Jesus.* So, be unwavering in your faith and consistent in reaching out to Him. He never gets tired of your requests; He has time for every single one of them.

We might be misdirected by people, by demands of the world, and by materialistic luster, but Jesus never changes His direction. His eyes are always pointed toward us. He knows our deepest cares and not only restores but also honors and crowns us with His glory. Hallelujah! She believed, and she was healed. We believe; therefore, we are healed.

OUR PROMISE

COMES THROUGH

THE CROWDS AND

crowns

US.

GOD CAN POUR ON THE BLESSINGS IN
ASTONISHING WAYS SO THAT YOU'RE
READY FOR ANYTHING AND EVERYTHING,
MORE THAN JUST READY TO DO WHAT
NEEDS TO BE DONE. AS ONE PSALMIST
PUTS IT, HE THROWS CAUTION TO THE
WINDS, GIVING TO THE NEEDY IN RECKLESS
ABANDON. HIS RIGHT-LIVING, RIGHT-GIVING
WAYS NEVER RUN OUT, NEVER WEAR OUT.
THIS MOST GENEROUS GOD WHO
GIVES SEED TO THE FARMER

THAT BECOMES BREAD FOR YOUR
MEALS IS MORE THAN EXTRAVAGANT
WITH YOU. HE GIVES YOU SOMETHING
YOU CAN THEN GIVE AWAY, WHICH
GROWS INTO FULL-FORMED LIVES,
ROBUST IN GOD, WEALTHY IN EVERY
WAY, SO THAT YOU CAN BE GENEROUS IN
EVERY WAY, PRODUCING WITH US
GREAT PRAISE TO GOD.

2 CORINTHIANS 9:8–11, MSG

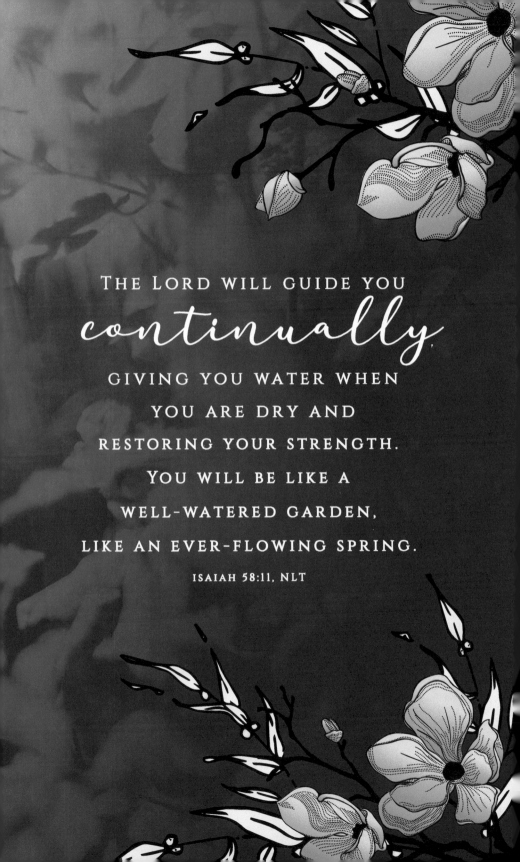

THE LORD WILL GUIDE YOU
continually,
GIVING YOU WATER WHEN
YOU ARE DRY AND
RESTORING YOUR STRENGTH.
YOU WILL BE LIKE A
WELL-WATERED GARDEN,
LIKE AN EVER-FLOWING SPRING.

ISAIAH 58:11, NLT

CONCLUSION

All you fabulous women, don't let the world tell you that you're just a woman. No, never! You're not! You are blessed, beautiful, precious, cared for, known, treasured, valued, purposed, worthy, and, more importantly, you are His beloved daughter! I would love for us to read together the following scripture portion because it sums up who we are in Christ Jesus.

CHRIST HOLDS IT ALL TOGETHER

WE LOOK AT THIS SON AND SEE THE GOD WHO CANNOT BE SEEN. WE LOOK AT THIS SON AND SEE GOD'S ORIGINAL PURPOSE IN EVERYTHING CREATED. FOR EVERYTHING, ABSOLUTELY EVERYTHING, ABOVE AND BELOW, VISIBLE AND INVISIBLE, RANK AFTER RANK AFTER RANK OF ANGELS—EVERYTHING GOT STARTED IN HIM AND FINDS ITS PURPOSE IN HIM. HE WAS THERE BEFORE ANY OF IT CAME INTO EXISTENCE AND HOLDS IT ALL TOGETHER RIGHT UP TO THIS MOMENT. AND WHEN IT COMES TO THE CHURCH, HE ORGANIZES AND HOLDS

IT TOGETHER, LIKE A HEAD DOES A BODY. HE WAS SU-
PREME IN THE BEGINNING AND—LEADING THE RESUR-
RECTION PARADE—HE IS SUPREME IN THE END. FROM
BEGINNING TO END HE'S THERE, TOWERING FAR ABOVE
EVERYTHING, EVERYONE. SO SPACIOUS IS HE, SO
ROOMY, THAT EVERYTHING OF GOD FINDS ITS PROP-
ER PLACE IN HIM WITHOUT CROWDING. NOT ONLY
THAT, BUT ALL THE BROKEN AND DISLOCATED PIEC-
ES OF THE UNIVERSE—PEOPLE AND THINGS, ANIMALS
AND ATOMS—GET PROPERLY FIXED AND FIT TOGETH-
ER IN VIBRANT HARMONIES, ALL BECAUSE OF HIS
DEATH, HIS BLOOD THAT POURED DOWN FROM THE
CROSS. YOU YOURSELVES ARE A CASE STUDY OF WHAT
HE DOES...BUT NOW, BY GIVING HIMSELF COMPLETE-
LY AT THE CROSS, ACTUALLY DYING FOR YOU, CHRIST
BROUGHT YOU OVER TO GOD'S SIDE AND PUT YOUR
LIVES TOGETHER, WHOLE AND HOLY IN HIS PRES-
ENCE. YOU DON'T WALK AWAY FROM A GIFT LIKE THAT!
YOU STAY GROUNDED AND STEADY IN THAT BOND OF
TRUST, CONSTANTLY TUNED IN TO THE MESSAGE...

COLOSSIANS 1:15-23, MSG

We might be broken, but not destroyed. Jesus will restore us piece by piece. He will hold all of our broken pieces in His hands, fix them beautifully, and fit each of them together in perfect harmony. Don't ever think it's the end, for there's always a restart with Jesus. He knows how to shape, grow, mature, and present you in this world. You're already seated in the heavenly places along with Jesus. You're positioned in His grace, and you will flourish no matter what! Don't walk away from His loving embrace but come, come as you are, and He will give you what you haven't even asked for because you mean the world to Him.

I speak blessings over every single one of you. May the love and grace of Jesus pour out into your lives. Even as you have read this book, I believe that the spirit of the Lord speaks to you in a special way about your identity and your worth. Just hold onto those words because they will hold true for your entire life. Jesus is living in you and is always with you. May His spirit lead you, guide you, speak to you, and grant you *Shalom*! Amen!

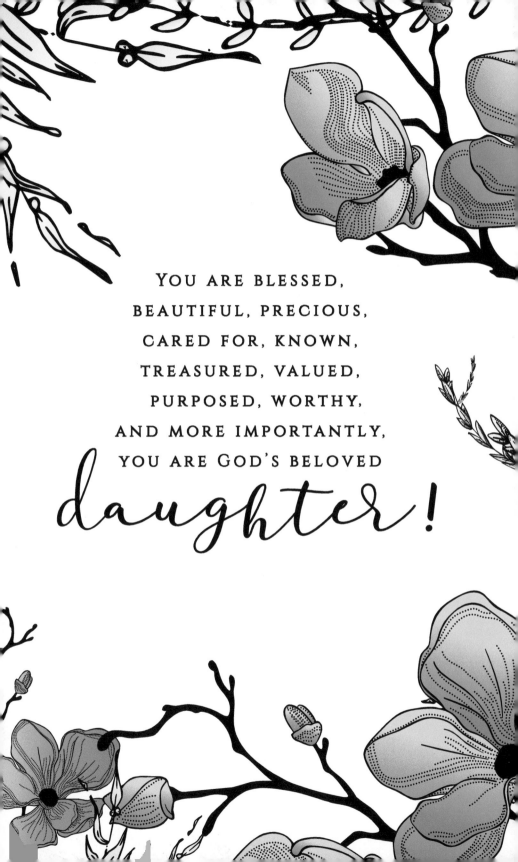

YOU ARE BLESSED,
BEAUTIFUL, PRECIOUS,
CARED FOR, KNOWN,
TREASURED, VALUED,
PURPOSED, WORTHY,
AND MORE IMPORTANTLY,
YOU ARE GOD'S BELOVED
daughter!

CPSIA information can be obtained
at www.ICGtesting.com
Printed in the USA
BVHW022210200820
586962BV00008B/215